Move It!

T0011530

by Wiley Blevins

LOOK!
BOOKS™

Red Chair Press   Egremont, Massachusetts

Look! Books are produced and published by Red Chair Press:

Red Chair Press LLC   PO Box 333   South Egremont, MA 01258-0333

FREE Educator Guides at www.redchairpress.com/free-resources

Publisher's Cataloging-In-Publication Data

Names: Blevins, Wiley, author.

Title: Move it! / by Wiley Blevins.

Description: Egremont, Massachusetts : Red Chair Press, [2021] | Series: Look! books : What a job | Interest age level: 005-008. | Includes index and resources for additional reading. | Summary: "In this book, readers discover what it takes to have a job where workers are responsible for moving things and people from one place to another, such as truck drivers, train and subway drivers"--Provided by publisher.

Identifiers: ISBN 9781634408301 (library hardcover) | ISBN 9781634408349 (paperback) | ISBN 9781634408387 (ebook)

Subjects: LCSH: Transportation--Vocational guidance--Juvenile literature. | Motor vehicle driving--Vocational guidance--Juvenile literature. | Locomotive engineers--Vocational guidance--Juvenile literature. | CYAC: Transportation--Vocational guidance. | Motor vehicle driving--Vocational guidance. | Locomotive engineers--Vocational guidance.

Classification: LCC HE152 .B54 2021 (print) | LCC HE152 (ebook) | DDC 388.023 [E]--dc23

Photo credits: Shutterstock except for the following: pp. Cover, 1, 15, 16, 18, 22: iStock; p. 5: Godong/Alamy; p. 11: Justin Kase zsixz/Alamy: p. 13: Paul Gregg Travel NZ/Alamy

Printed in United States of America

0920   1P   CGS21

Table of Contents

At some jobs a person sits or stands most of the day. But at other jobs people really have to move it! Are you up to the task of these busy jobs?

Trapeze Artist

This job has a lot of twists and spins. Trapeze artists often **perform** one or two times a day. It's like flying without wings. But first, they must get ready. They put on make-up. They dress in colorful costumes. They warm up with handstands and push-ups.

Good to Know

A gymnast makes a great trapeze artist. You have to be strong and light. And you can't be afraid!

Astronaut

Up, up, and away. An astronaut zooms into space. The astronaut has lots of work to do. Some astronauts work on the space station. Others do **experiments** to learn new things. The astronaut must wear special clothes.

Before flying into space, astronauts get lots of training. Where? On Earth. They practice in a **simulator**. It helps them feel what being in space is like.

8

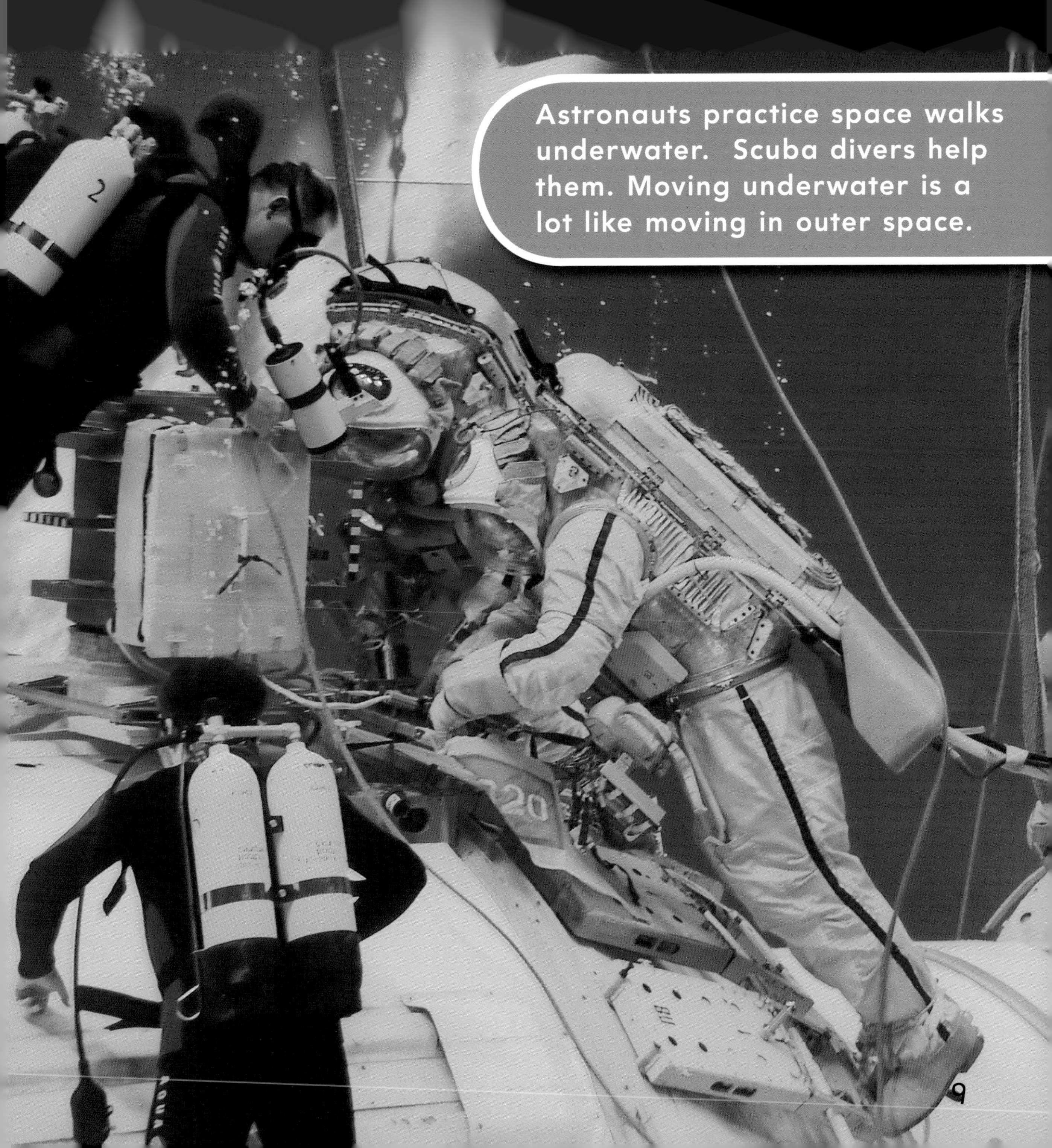

Astronauts practice space walks underwater. Scuba divers help them. Moving underwater is a lot like moving in outer space.

House Mover

Can a house go from one place to another? It can! But you have to call a house mover. Big houses. Little houses. All move in one or two big pieces. You can even leave everything inside!

Good to Know

People have always moved their homes. Tents. Teepees. Yurts. And more!

It can cost less to move a house than to buy a new one. The house is put on a **dolly** with wheels. Then it is driven to a new place. How? Slowly. Very, very slowly.

Bike Tour Guide

This job is a great way to see the world and get lots of exercise. Bike tour guides lead trips on two wheels. Pedal. Pedal. Glide. In a city. Through the country. Up and down a mountain trail.

Bike tour guides must be in good physical shape to ride and ride.

A bike trip can last a weekend. A week. Or a month. To be a good guide, you must be a friendly person. You must also know a lot about the place you are going.

Mail Pilot

How does your mail get from one place to the next fast? Some mail is flown in a plane. By whom? A mail pilot. Mail and packages move across the country overnight.

Good to Know

Small planes can go to smaller places far away from big cities.

Flight Attendant

Pilots aren't the only workers on a plane. Flight attendants have an important job. They make sure the people on the plane are safe. If an **emergency** happens, they are trained to stay calm and help.

Pilots and flight attendants
aren't the only workers
to move people. Train
conductors and bus and taxi
drivers also move people.
People and things
are always on
the move!

Words to Know

dolly: a low truck or cart with wheels

emergency: a sudden event for which you need help fast

experiments: tests to learn something new

perform: to act, like in a play or show

simulator: a machine used for training workers before they face real conditions

Learn More at the Library

Check out these books to learn more.

McCarthy, Meghan. *Astronaut Handbook.* Dragonfly Books, 2017.

Ysidro, Carol. *Robby Learns to Fly.* Sweet Pea Publishing, 2018.

Mattern, Joanne. *We Go on an Airplane.* Red Chair Press, 2020.

Index

About the Author

Wiley Blevins is on the job as a writer and editor in New York. He gets to his job with the help of people on the move, such as the train conductor and subway driver.